AMERICAN RUINS

AMERICAN RUINS

PHOTOGRAPHS BY ARTHUR DROOKER

FOREWORD BY DOUGLAS BRINKLEY ESSAY BY CHRISTOPHER WOODWARD

MERRELL
LONDON · NEW YORK

Published by

Merrell Publishers Limited

81 Southwark Street

London SE1 0HX

merrellpublishers.com

First published 2007

Paperback edition first published 2009

British Library Cataloguing-in-Publication Data:
Drooker, Arthur.
   American ruins.
   1. Drooker, Arthur. 2. Ruined buildings – United States –
   Pictorial works. 3. United States – Antiquities – Pictorial
   works.
   I. Title II. Woodward, Christopher.
   779.4′473′092-dc22

ISBN 978-1-8589-4497-5

Developed and produced by Gary Chassman,
Verve Editions

verveeditions.com

Designed by Kari Finkler
Copyedited by Elizabeth S. Shanley
Printed and bound in China

For more information on original prints, please visit
americanruinsbook.com.

Front cover John S. Cook Bank, Rhyolite, Nevada
Back cover Windsor, Alcorn, Mississippi
pg. 2 Windsor, Alcorn, Mississippi
pg. 5 Sheldon Church, Gardens Corner, South Carolina
pg. 6 Mission San Jose, San Antonio, Texas
pg. 15 Image courtesy of Library of Congress, Prints &
Photographs Division [LC-DIG-Stereo-IS00363]
pg. 16 Images © Ed Ruscha. Courtesy of Gagosian
Gallery, New York. Photography by Paul Ruscha.

NOTES

"In the Region of Romance and Fancy"
by Arthur Drooker

1. James Henry Carleton, "Diary of an excursion to the
ruins of Abo, Quarra, and Gran Quivira, in New Mexico
under the command of Major James Henry Carleton,
U.S.A.," *Ninth Annual Report of the Board of Regents of
the Smithsonian Institution* (Washington, DC: Beverly
Tucker, Senate Printer, 1855).

"Arthur Drooker's *American Ruins*"
by Christopher Woodward

1. Zeph. 2:13.

2. Beaumont Newhall, preface to *Photographic Views
of Sherman's Campaign,* by George N. Barnard (New
York: Dover Publications, 1977), xvii.

3. Charles Dickens, *Pictures from Italy* (London:
Bradbury & Evans, 1846).

4. R. A. McNeal, ed., *Nicholas Biddle in Greece: The
Journals and Letters of 1806* (Philadelphia: Pennsylvania
State University Press, 1993).

5. Audrey J. Horning, "Shenandoah's Secret History,"
Archaeology, January–February 2000.

6. Arthur Drooker's Web site, "Machu Picchu
Portfolio," http://www.drookerphotography.com/.

7. Carleton, "Diary of an excursion."

8. Vincent Scully, *American Architecture and Urbanism*
(London: Thames & Hudson, 1969), 24.

9. Thomas Jefferson to Madame de Tessé, Nîmes,
20 March 1787, in *Jefferson Abroad,* ed. Douglas Wilson
and Lucia Stanton (New York: Modern Library, 1999), 132.

10. McNeal, *Nicholas Biddle in Greece.*

11. Scully, *American Architecture and Urbanism,* 71.

12. M. T. Anderson, conversation with author,
March 2007.

13. Horace Walpole to Sir Horace Mann, 24 November
1774, in *The Yale Editions of Horace Walpole's
Correspondence*, ed. George L. Lam, W. S. Lewis, and
Warren Hunting Smith (New Haven: Yale University
Press, 1967), 24:62.

14. Ed Ruscha and Donna M. De Salvo, *Ed Ruscha:
Course of Empire*, foreword by Joan Didion (Ostfildern-
Ruit: Hatje Cantz, 2005), an exhibition catalogue.

15. Director of The Greening of Detroit, conversation
with author, May 2007.

16. Andrew Sinclair, *Jack: A Biography of Jack London*
(London: Weidenfeld & Nicolson, 1978), 193.

17. Jack London to Joan London, 24 February 1914, in
*Letters from Jack London; Containing an Unpublished
Correspondence Between London and Sinclair Lewis,*
ed. King Hendricks and Irving Shepard (London:
MacGibbon & Kee, 1966).

18. Henry James, *Italian Hours* (London: William
Heinemann, 1909).

Rosewell

1. Jefferson to John Page, 20 July 1776, in *The Eye
of Thomas Jefferson*, ed. William Howard Adams
(Washington, DC: National Gallery of Art, 1976).

2. Fred Carter, letter to the editor, *Newport News Daily
Press*, 2 June 2002.

Rhyolite

1. Louis Wittig's Web site, "Unpublished Masterpieces,"
http://louiswittig.com/unpubsamples/Rhyolite.htm.

Wolf House

1. Jack London, quoted in the permanent exhibition
shown at the House of Happy Walls in the Jack
London State Historic Park in Glen Ellen, California.

Knapp's Castle

1. Raymond Ford, "Knapp's Castle," Santa Barbara
Outdoors,
http://www.sb-outdoors.org/Trails/index3.php/?ID=51.

FOR HUCK AND EL

CONTENTS

FOREWORD

BY DOUGLAS BRINKLEY

Pueblo Bonito, Chaco Canyon, New Mexico

NATURALLY, IT HAPPENED ON THEODORE ROOSEVELT'S WATCH. The Antiquities Act of 1906 declared the protection of American ruins as a federal measure to deter artifact thieves. Roosevelt understood that ruins were essentially windows to understanding the past. Fascinated by prehistoric cultures in the Southwest, he hoped the ruins there—being pilfered by pot hunters—would become touchstone places for his fellow Americans, something akin to Stonehenge in England or the Great Wall in China.

One archaeological site in particular—Chaco Canyon, a major urban center of ancestral Puebloan culture located in New Mexico—transfixed Roosevelt. Studying photographs of these ruins allowed his imagination to plunge backward in time. Roosevelt was amazed that Chaco Canyon had ceremonial buildings and engineering projects of great sophistication, and just seeing the austere rubble transported him to a prehistoric time when the Four Corners region was bustling with human life, a true crossroads of civilization.

With the Antiquities Act, Roosevelt saved Chaco Canyon for posterity to enjoy. Photographer Arthur Drooker does the same (in a different medium from politics) with his fine, ethereal ruins images published in this elegant book. Crisscrossing America, camera in hand, carefully gauging light, Drooker found beauty in the abandoned and forlorn. Some of the places he visited are iconic sites, such as Harpers Ferry, West Virginia, and Alcatraz Island, California. But most are forgotten sentinels from a distant era, bathed in the mystique of ancient footsteps. You can almost hear the echo of slavery's whip in Drooker's photo of Windsor Plantation in Mississippi or feel the inferno that destroyed Jack London's Wolf House in California. All the historical clamor, however, is now gone. What's left is tranquility. That is what Drooker captures best.

Although Drooker means this book to be a "celebration" of ruins, I also feel loss as I flip through the pages and read the text. These days, as I wander around New Orleans, new ruins spring up like mushrooms. What was once the home of the Fultons or the Boudreauxs now has a big Day-Glo X spray-painted on the front door, accompanied by the word "condemned" posted on the porch. Given global warming and chemical weapons and nuclear reactors, you wonder whether everyplace might someday become a candidate for Drooker's ruins portfolio.

But, alas, Drooker's images provide relief. Nature has reclaimed many of these weathered buildings: moss and weeds and tall grasses sweep over the old stones with a profound grace. The spirit harbored in these photographs, to my mind, is that, in the end, nature wins. That is comforting. For that reason alone, I find Drooker's vision as soothing as the cool repetition of ocean waves. His art is a gift to Old Time America.

IN THE REGION OF ROMANCE AND FANCY

BY ARTHUR DROOKER

AMERICAN RUINS. THE PHRASE SOUNDS LIKE A CONTRADICTION. *American*, after all, has always represented what's new to the rest of the world; it's a synonym for the future, while *ruins* are the remains of a forgotten and obsolete past. But in remote areas barely noted on maps, far from the interstates, the malls, and the sprawl, there are places with crumbling walls and weathered facades that stand in defiance of time and progress. This book celebrates these places, these American ruins.

I was drawn to these sites to forge a spiritual connection with those who came before us, to capture the visual poetry of what they left behind, and restore what they had built to our collective memory.

To transform these aspirations into images, I shot in digital infrared format. The infrared band of light on the spectrum is invisible to the human eye, but a specially adapted digital camera can record it. What it sees is a spirit world of haunted beauty. Infrared light conjures up ethereal landscapes where shadows hover like apparitions, leaves and grass glow in downy white, clouds float in their own dreamy dimension, and ruins appear as fragments of an unsolvable mystery.

A ruin's potential as an infrared subject was just one of three criteria I employed in selecting which sites to include in this book. The sites also had to be preserved as ruins and protected as such by a public or private entity. Lastly, I sought places that, taken together, would create an eclectic but representative survey of America's rich architectural, historical, and geographical diversity.

As a photographic series, these images present a rare overview of some overlooked landmarks and allow us, as Americans, to see where we came from, measure how far we've come, and gain a vision of where we might be headed.

Ultimately, these areas of inquiry lack definitive conclusions. Like the ruins themselves, the answers remain incomplete and can never be fully known. But that is the lure of these places. Perhaps Major James Carleton, an officer in the U.S. Army, expressed it best. Leading an expedition through the Southwest in 1853, he came upon the adobe remains of Abo Mission in what is now New Mexico. His comments, though specific to this isolated religious outpost, could eloquently describe a visit to any site in this book:

> In the mystery that envelops everything connected with these ruins, there is much food for very interesting speculation. Until that mystery is penetrated . . . Abo belongs to the region of romance and fancy and it will be for the poet and the painter to restore to its original beauty this venerable temple.[1]

Photography was in its infancy when Major Carleton visited Abo Mission. Had he known of this new medium, he might have amended his comments to add that it's for the photographer to preserve "the region of romance and fancy" where such places as Abo really reside. More than a century and a half later, I hope I've accomplished the task.

ARTHUR DROOKER'S *AMERICAN RUINS*

BY CHRISTOPHER WOODWARD

AMERICAN RUINS IS A PHOTOGRAPHIC EPIC.
No artist before Arthur Drooker has undertaken such a journey
to the ruins of the United States, from Hawaii to Florida and
from the Hudson River to New Mexico. The pictures span the
centuries: the majority of these ruins date from the eighteenth
and nineteenth centuries, but several are older, and only one—
that of the U.S. Penitentiary at Alcatraz—postdates the First
World War. This book is also an epic because Drooker shows
architecture at its most ambitious. What, his pictures ask,
do ruins tell us about the aspirations of the people who built
these structures? And if architecture outlasts us—and the stones
of Pueblo Bonito were put into place more than a thousand years
ago—what will our buildings tell future travelers about the way
we live? To Drooker, the ruins in this book "allow us, as Americans,
to see where we came from, measure how far we've come, and
gain a vision of where we might be headed."

Is it possible to tell the story of the United States through its
ruins? Apparently not. Even the San Francisco earthquake of 1906
is not memorialized by a single ruin today. But is it possible
to tell the story without the ruins pictured in this book?

▪ ▪ ▪

In his poem "To the United States" (1827), one of the great eulogies
to the idea of America, Goethe imagined a continent without the
shadow of ruins:

> *America, you have it better*
> *Than our old continent;*
> *You have no ruined castles*
> *And no primordial stones.*
> *Your soul, your inner life*
> *Remain untroubled by*
> *Useless memory*
> *And wasted strife.*

In Europe, however, the life of the living was overshadowed
by memories of a troubled, violent past. Goethe wrote at a time
of profound despair, when, in consequence of the French
Revolution, a fragmented pessimism had replaced the expansive
optimism of the Enlightenment. It was a period in which idealists
abandoned a Europe that they believed to be irredeemably
corrupt and contaminated: such men as the scientist Joseph
Priestley, the social visionary Robert Owen, and the poet Samuel
Taylor Coleridge placed their hopes in the new republic. Mary
Shelley's novel *The Last Man* (1826) imagined Europe devastated
by a plague in the year AD 2100. Its hero walks to Rome, hoping

that any fellow survivors will make their way to that pivot of European consciousness. But Rome, too, is deserted, and he sails down the Tiber toward the Atlantic and the New World. To many of Shelley's generation, America was an escape from the inevitable decay in Europe.

Only three years later, however, Thomas Cole conceived the first great work of American art to be inspired by ruins: *The Course of Empire.* In 1829 the landscape painter returned to Europe to study—his parents had emigrated from Britain when he was seventeen—and as he explored London he wrote in his notebook an idea: "the epitome of man." Next he traveled to Rome, and it was as he watched a sunset over the Colosseum—so his first biographer, Lewis Noble, tells us—that he imagined a series of pictures that would depict the rise and fall of human civilization. The first of five he painted—today in the collection of the New-York Historical Society—shows a wilderness at dawn. The second shows Arcadia; by noon it is an imperial city of dazzling marble monuments; next, the city is sacked and burned; and the sun sets on a "Desolation" in which the only souvenir of the empire is a single column on top of which storks nest. Travel, asserted Cole, should have a moral purpose, and *The Course of Empire* warned of what might happen if his adopted country abandoned the values of its founders. It would repeat the European experience summarized in the lines from Byron's *Childe Harold's Pilgrimage* (1818) with which Cole advertised the exhibit: "First Freedom, and then Glory – when that fails, / Wealth, vice, corruption, – barbarism at last."

America was not, of course, as untroubled as in Goethe's eulogy. In the 1830s the Bulow Plantation in Florida was destroyed by Seminole warriors. The old Sheldon Church in Gardens Corner, South Carolina, was one of many structures burned in the War of Independence. The Abo Mission already cast a long shadow on the desert; it had been abandoned in the seventeenth century. And while Cole prepared his canvases for exhibition, the city around him burned in the Great Fire of New York of 1835.

That fire was painted by several observers, but the first iconic images of real—as opposed to imagined—American ruins are in George Barnard's *Photographic Views of Sherman's Campaign,* published in 1886, after the end of the Civil War. Barnard had traveled with Sherman's army, and the majority of the views are of incidents in the landscape: timber emplacements and woods with trees split by cannon. However, Barnard also photographed the sacked cities of Columbia and Charleston, South Carolina. The Doric arcades of the railway depot at Charleston—set fire to by the "rebels" in their retreat—recede like the arches of an

George N. Barnard, *Ruins in Charleston, S.C.*, 1863 or 1864.
Albumen print, 10 1/8 × 14 1/8 in (25.7 × 35.9 cm).
San Francisco Museum of Modern Art.

aqueduct in the Roman Campagna; in Columbia the plaster has fallen from the portico of Mr. Pinckney's house, and the brick columns are hatched as black as the darkest of Piranesi engravings. To an educated audience—and Barnard's book sold for $100—the comparison with pictures of antiquity must have been inescapable.

Arthur Drooker is a photographer who admires good architecture and cites as his heroes the nineteenth-century artists and photographers Francis Frith, William James Stillman, and Frederick Catherwood. Each was a traveler; each could combine a picturesque composition with precise architectural information. The same applies to Drooker. We see this in Sheldon Church, which was rebuilt but burned a second time, by Sherman in 1865. In Drooker's photographs its ruin might be a Roman temple in the woods. But we also admire the proportions of the architect's design for the colonnade, and the symmetry of the elevations.

Barnard was also the first to show how easily—and how seductively—black-and-white photography can metamorphose ruins into objects of beauty. In Drooker's photographs the same dilemma is presented. The buildings in this book are ruins because of fire and poverty, earthquakes and war. Why do we enjoy looking at them?

∎ ∎ ∎

In the booklet he wrote to explain his pictures, George Barnard did not draw any moral lessons from the scenes he witnessed. Others did moralize on the devastation of the Civil War, however, continuing a tradition that is as old as the Bible. In the book of Zephaniah, ruin is the punishment prophesied for Nineveh: God will make it "a desolation, and dry like a wilderness . . . The cormorant and the bittern shall lodge in the upper lintels of it; their voice shall sing in the windows; desolation shall be in the thresholds."[1]

A unionist journalist described Charleston in 1866 as follows: "A city of ruins, of desolation, of vacant houses, of widowed women, of rotting wharves, of deserted warehouses, of weed-wild gardens, of miles of grass-grown streets, of acres of pitiful and voiceful barrenness – that is Charleston, wherein Rebellion loftily reared its head five years ago."[2] The words were chosen to echo the words of the Bible. As with Nineveh, the desolation of Charleston represents a moral judgment upon its inhabitants. In 1865 author Taylor Lewis called the book he published on the charred South *State Rights: A Photograph from the Ruins of Ancient Greece.* "God has given us a mirror into the past," Lewis wrote, claiming that all the troubles of ancient Greece were the consequence of individual states' wishes to be independent from their federation.

Do we still read moral lessons into the ruins we visit? In Rome, at least, the practice ended in the nineteenth century. But Arthur Drooker is trying to revive this approach—and why not? Take Bannerman Castle, on an island in the Hudson. It was built at the beginning of the twentieth century by Francis Bannerman, an immigrant from Scotland who became rich by buying and selling surplus military hardware at the end of the Civil War. He bought Pollepel Island as a safe place to store explosives. The castle's function was to be an arsenal, but it was designed by Bannerman to look like a structure from his home country's mythical past. He would be a controversial figure today—a dealer in secondhand arms whose goods blew off heads and pierced flesh as far away as Asia—but he romanticized himself by the construction of this folly.

Visiting the Colosseum in 1846, Charles Dickens was unable to separate his experience of the structure from his knowledge of the martyrdom of Christians in the arena. As he climbed the terraces, the stones crunched and separated underfoot; Dickens wrote that the structure should continue to crumble one inch per year, so that it demonstrated the destruction of paganism. "God be thanked: a ruin!" he declared from its summit.[3] Should we say the same at Bannerman Castle, as the arms dealer's turrets and pinnacles crumble year by year into the vegetation? The question is not whether we think Bannerman a good man or a bad man, but whether that debate should be in the mind of the modern visitor to ruins.

∎ ∎ ∎

But do such ruins tell the truth about the past? The very first American traveler to make the analogy between America and ancient Greece was Nicholas Biddle. He visited Athens in 1804, at the age of nineteen—the second American citizen ever to do so. The ruins inspired him to become a statesman, as their magnificence demonstrated the power of oratory, debate, and words. Sparta, by contrast, was an empty plain, and its disappearance gave "a Republican a melancholy pleasure. My own country offers an interesting analogy of which I have thought much . . . It is thus we are instructed in the melancholy but pleasing philosophy of ruins."[4]

However, Biddle had not read his Thucydides. Writing in the fifth century BC, the historian noted that if Sparta "became deserted . . . future generations would, as time passed, find it very difficult to believe that the place had really been as powerful" as it was in reality, because its soldier-rulers spent little money on monuments— hence, it quickly became that empty plain. Athens, by contrast, would seem twice as powerful as it was because of its lavish expenditure on monuments. Biddle was deceived.

But ruins can also do the opposite and reveal a truth disguised by books and official images. A fascinating article from 2000 by Audrey J. Horning in *Archaeology*—so fascinating that I stole the journal from a hotel at the ruins of Uxmal in the Yucatan— described a project in the Shenandoah Valley of Virginia.[5] Archaeologists studied 2,500 acres (1,000 ha) of land from which 460 people were expelled in the 1930s in order to create a national park. At the time, sociologists described the inhabitants as "families of unlettered folk, of almost pure Anglo-Saxon stock, sheltered in tiny, mud-plastered log cabins and supported by a primitive agriculture . . . The ragged children, until 1928, never had seen the flag or heard of the Lord's Prayer; the community is almost completely cut off from the current of American life." This perceived backwardness justified their relocation by the state and the destruction of their homes.

But excavations uncovered such objects as a Buck Rogers ray gun and a tattered Maxfield Parrish calendar. In the official publication a Mrs. Nicholson posed on her porch in an old-fashioned bonnet for the photographer Arthur Rothstein; inside, however—the dig discovered—she had a tea set of Japanese porcelain. Shenandoah was a far more complex and modern community than the state-sponsored sociologists and photographers had told the public in the 1930s.

Ruins will always be reinterpreted, and this openness to interpretation is one reason why the same structure can fascinate different generations of travelers. A ruin is by definition incomplete. We supply what has vanished from our own imaginations and memories, so a visit is a dialogue between an incomplete reality and the ideas and thoughts of the individual visitor. Drooker first understood this when, as a boy, his father showed him pictures from a visit to Machu Picchu. The Inca city has been studied and studied, but its original purpose continues to be a mystery: "The Incas never told, proving that lost cities may be found, but they're never fully revealed. Not even in photographs . . . Its true identity will be as elusive as the mist which floats across the mountain-top," Drooker continues, "and that elusiveness is the lure of these places, a quality which the camera can capture."[6]

Drooker quotes Major James Carleton, whose expedition of 1853 came across the adobe ruins of the Abo Mission, New Mexico. "In the mystery that envelops everything connected with these ruins," Carleton wrote, "there is much food for very interesting speculation. Until that mystery is penetrated . . . Abo belongs to the region of romance and fancy and it will be for the poet and the painter to restore to its original beauty this venerable temple."[7] To Drooker, however, it is the purpose of the artist to celebrate that place in "romance and fancy." The potency of ruins is in what we think and feel, not in the facts we are told. Our engagement with them is imaginative, creative, and personal.

The most mysterious site in this book is Pueblo Bonito in Chaco Canyon, dated to between 850 and 1150, when the Pueblo civilization of the Southwest was at its most urban and monumental. We now know that the ruins are fragments of a great residential structure built in the shape of a D and five stories high. The courtyard was ceremonial, with cylindrical chambers rising above the ground. To one scholar of Pueblo civilization, Vincent Scully, we must nevertheless abandon ourselves to visions: "The old towns [surviving in the Mesa Verde] still seem to await the mask and the rattle and the feet pounding the drum of the earth, and in the modern pueblos the dance goes on."[8]

■ ■ ■

In the nineteenth century, photographs of these Native American structures were published by such photographers as Timothy O'Sullivan, who accompanied the military surveys of the Southwest in the 1870s. However, they did not sit very happily with the self-image of the nation; an image expressed in Neoclassical architecture since the time of Thomas Jefferson. Jefferson built the Capitol at Richmond, Virginia, as an exact replica of the Maison Carée at Nîmes, a Roman temple of the first century AD. In a letter to Madame de Tessé on March 20, 1787, he described himself "gazing whole hours . . . at the Temple, like a lover at his mistress": the local weavers "consider me an [sic] hypochondriac Englishman, about to write with a pistol, the last chapter of his history."[9] Jefferson's joke is at the expense of the British Romantics, for whom ruins had become projections of their own personal despair, analogies for doubt and neurosis. He wanted to build monuments, not meditate on ruins, and so the Capitol at Richmond was not a homage to ruin but replicated the perfection of the original design.

Timothy H. O'Sullivan, *Ruins in Cañon de Chelle, N.M., in a Cavity in the Wall, 60 Feet Above Present Bed of Cañon*, 1873. Photographic print on stereo card: stereograph, albumen.

It was Nicholas Biddle—dubbed "Nick the Greek"—who in the early nineteenth century popularized the Greek Revival architectural style in the United States. Born in 1786 to one of the leading families in New England, he was one of the generation that inherited Jefferson's expectations of the new republic. In Europe—on that journey as a nineteen-year-old—he had little interest in its modern cities: the "coming people" of Pennsylvania, he wrote, would be "more civilised, more enlightened, better than any of these whose exploits are transmitted by history . . ."[10] It was in Athens—not Rome—that he found the raw materials of antiquity, untouched by later hands. The city was little visited, squalid, depopulated, and idle under the occupation of the Turks. In consequence, Biddle was able to claim ownership of the ruins for America. The marble fragments would be the building blocks for a new society.

Jefferson and Biddle take us to Windsor in Alcorn, Mississippi, and the Cottage near Plaquemine, Louisiana; both great Neoclassical mansions of the nineteenth century. Vincent Scully has noted that the model of the Classical temple—as seen at Richmond—lasted longest in the planters' houses in the states of the South. The timelessness of the style was an assertion of values in contrast to the industrial cities of the North: "Their softly gleaming column screens furnished the symbolic image around which Southern apologetics of the immediately pre-Civil War period and . . . mythology of the interminably postwar period were both to be fashioned."[11] And it is the ruined plantation houses that are the most powerful expression of this ideal: "The more in ruin, the more Greek they seemed," continues Scully; without kitchens, or chandeliers, or carriage lamps, they are closer to their Classical models. In addition, these two ruins are fixed at one moment in time, and we can project on these structures what we want to see. Windsor and the Cottage have become symbols of a world that has vanished—and whether that it is a good thing or not depends on where the traveler has come from.

■ ■ ■

Jefferson and Biddle also take us to Bethlehem, Pennsylvania: the site of one of only two modern ruins in this book. Of all the industrial ruins in the States, it is this gigantic steel mill that has become *the* symbol of national decline and the challenges of the globalized world. In its first decades, the mill was celebrated as a symbol of power. The steel for such American icons as the Empire State Building and the Golden Gate Bridge was made here. In the 1950s its chief executive was the best paid in the nation. But the

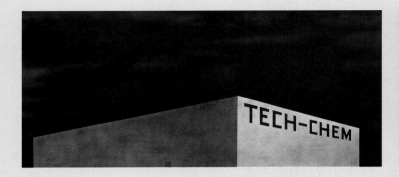

Ed Ruscha, *Blue Collar Tech-Chem*, 1992. Acrylic on canvas.

Ed Ruscha, *The Old Tech-Chem Building*, 2005. Acrylic on canvas.

company was bankrupted in 2001, and—in large part, because of foreign competition—the mill has closed. Its assets are now owned by an Indian steel conglomerate, and the site will be reused as a casino. To the novelist M. T. Anderson, stories such as this symbolize how in the years after the Second World War, "America has changed from a country which glorified production to a country which glorifies consumption."[12]

In earlier centuries, ruins have symbolized the doubts of empires about their own future. In the aftermath of the Seven Years' War (1756–63), Britain began to speak of itself as "the new Rome," but as early as the War of Independence it began to imagine its ruin. In 1774 Horace Walpole wrote: "The next Augustan age will dawn on the other side of the Atlantic. There will, perhaps, be a Thucydides at Boston and a Xenophon in New York . . . At last, some curious traveller from Lima will visit England and give a description of the ruins of St Paul's, like the editions of Palmyra and Balbec . . ."[13] In the 1830s the architect John Soane imagined his masterpiece, the Bank of England, as a ruin of the future, excavated by archaeologists from such a future civilization. Rome, Carthage, Athens, Memphis, and Troy . . . why not London?

The United States has added its own twist to the metaphor. Perhaps the most striking single image of ruin in recent decades is the discovery of the Statue of Liberty at the end of the film *Planet of the Apes* (1968). Half-buried in the sand, the torch and tablet fractured, that piece of set design captured the period's fear of the impact of a nuclear war. In 2005 the American exhibit at the Venice Biennale was *Course of Empire* by Ed Ruscha, a conscious response to Cole's cycle. Ruscha painted warehouses, kiosks, and parking lots in Los Angeles, showing how the topography has changed radically in little more than a decade. He explained, "It's kind of awesome to imagine that everything has to go through its lifestyle and to visualize everything that might encompass and to know that nothing lasts. There are people who imagine how the world goes and that things actually get better . . . I don't view things quite that way."[14] That pessimism—the acceptance that things *don't* actually get better—is Ruscha's laconic update of Cole's doubts about the progress of man.

The new office blocks in Silicon Valley are built to be as anonymous and flexible as possible, able to be let to a diversity of temporary owners. Only the logos change. That is a pragmatic response, of course, to the reality of an economy that can put up bigger structures than ever before, more quickly than ever before—and abandon them more quickly than ever before.

But what will the buildings we erect today tell future peoples about the aspirations of our culture? Although Drooker has lived in Los Angeles for thirty years and has often photographed its architecture in the medium of infrared, he does not comment explicitly. But his pictures invite us to ask the question.

■　■　■

"They're the wrong kind of ruins," a cab driver told me in Detroit. I explained that I had written a book about ruins several years ago, and that this trip was to help me understand why the greatest contemporary interest in the subject was in the States, that paradigm of modernity. I had come to see the ruins of the Beaux-Arts skyscrapers, Modernist factories, and bourgeois mansions erected in the first decades of the twentieth century. But I was not prepared for a city in which fifteen minutes' walk from the Hilton Hotel an empty house plot can be bought for $50.[15] Wild pheasants flap in the silent concrete shells of old factories, and beech trees grow thirty feet high on the roof of a burned post office. Seventy years ago this was one of the richest cities in the world. Within a few decades the city's population has fallen from two million to half a million, the fastest decline of any Western city since Rome in the fifth century AD.

To a European, it is the transience of American communities that is most startling: our European tradition of prophesying future ruin did not imagine the phenomenon of the "shrinking city"— or the "ghost town." Driving through Boulder, Colorado, last year, I looked for the site of the town of Tungsten. During the First World War, tungsten metal became more valuable than gold and silver, and twenty thousand people lived there. Today, there is nothing—not a shack. For an Englishman, such transience is hard to comprehend. America did not invent the ghost town, true, but it was the first to romanticize such places.

In *American Ruins*, ghost towns are represented by Rhyolite, founded in the Nevada gold rush of 1904. Three years later, the boomtown had more than ten thousand people, a school, a train station, electric streetlight twenty-four hours a day, and a bank with a safe that could hold a million dollars in gold coins. But the prospectors moved on, and two years later, Rhyolite's population was fewer than a thousand and the lights were turned off.

From hundreds of ghost towns, Drooker chose Rhyolite, I think, because of the stature of the Cook Bank. By the turn of the twentieth century, banks had become the monuments on Main Street, as in the masterpieces built in that same decade of the 1900s by Louis Sullivan in the agricultural states of Wisconsin and Minnesota. The Cook Bank is a simple concrete shell, but its facade is as upright and assertive as a billboard—and in Drooker's photograph somehow magnificent and proud.

■　■　■

From the ghost town, it is a short step to the empty house on the prairie. Fewer than one in a hundred Americans lives on a farm today, but once upon a time, however, half did. In consequence, that old wooden house has its place in the ancestral sense of self of millions of modern city-dwellers. Interestingly, Drooker ignores this theme. It has been "done" by other artists—among them Maxwell MacKenzie in Minnesota, the Dakotas, and Montana—but, more importantly, he is interested in architecture that expresses dreams, aspirations, and ambitions. He photographs Dungeness, a Gilded Age mansion left to rot— a modern *vanitas*—and Jack London's Wolf House in California, burned in the winter of 1913, just one month before its construction was due to finish. Wolf House has the most interesting story to tell.

Beginning in 1911, thirty men worked for two years to construct the walls of London's ranch house, made from hand-scoured volcanic stone. By this date London earned over $70,000 a year, typing thousands of words late into each night. He had come to despise the mechanics of authorship, but he wrote, he said, to pay for the ranch and the house. When the fire happened, he was $100,000 in debt. He never had the money to rebuild.

The ruin illustrates the complexity of our personal relationship with ruins. "Wolf" was London's nickname for himself, and to Andrew Sinclair—the first of his modern biographers—London saw his own ruin in the fire-blackened walls.[16] In 1906 he had rushed to San Francisco to witness the city in flames, joining the hundreds of amateur photographers recording the scene—a phenomenon of spectatorship for which, incidentally, there was no precedent in Europe. London's photographs of the city hall had a personal significance, however. He had hoped that it would burn to the ground, as in its archives was the paper evidence of his illegitimate birth: his true father was an itinerant astrologer named John Chaney. When City Hall did disappear in flames, London was—to Sinclair—"born again."

London began Wolf House five years later, and it was designed to withstand an earthquake. However, it also crystallized the unresolved conflicts in his life. The spokesperson for socialism in America had left the slums to become a landowner. It was a family house for a man whose only children lived with his first wife. It coincided, too, with illness, alcoholism, and uncertainty. London never wrote directly about the fire—he refused to, even in letters to his second wife—and so he never tells us what thoughts he projected on to the smoke-blackened walls. Several months after the blaze, however, he wrote a letter to his thirteen-year-old daughter, Joan, in which he uses the word *ruin* time after time. The metaphor is of Joan as a colt: "You have been

ruined by your trainer, [her mother]: if I were dying I should not care to have you at my bedside. A ruined colt is a ruined colt, and I do not like ruined colts."[17]

The letter is uncharacteristic, and London was to be reconciled to Joan. Indeed, there was a happy ending—of sorts—at the ranch. London's few interludes of happiness in his troubled and sick last years were in watching the dry valley become a fertile, bountiful paradise. In 1912 he wrote the first novel to imagine the United States after an environmental disaster, *The Scarlet Plague*, an American sequel to Shelley's *The Last Man*. It begins with San Francisco as an archaeological site of the future: the site of a contest between man and a victorious nature. California is the setting of the second novel on this theme, *The Earth Abides*, written by George R. Stewart in 1949. This imagines a landscape that has regained its "state of biological grace"—as in the Arcadia painted by Cole—just ten years after the destruction of civilization. After twenty years, however, the Golden Gate Bridge is rusted. Next, the span falls into the water. The steel was manufactured at Bethlehem.

■ ■ ■

Visiting ruins in the countryside around Rome, Henry James commented that "the pleasure, I confess, shows a note of perversity."[18] Why did he linger in these piles of dead stones, he asked? As we have seen, a ruin is much more than a picturesque silhouette, or a dramatic contrast of light and shade. It is a place of spirit and atmosphere that invites us to think about the past, present, and future. But ruins can also be happy, uplifting places. Dead stones can come to life. How? If there is a magic formula, the most important ingredient is nature.

My favorite example is of the poet Percy Bysshe Shelley in Rome in 1818. He arrived in a state of despair, depressed by a Europe where—in his view—every country was in the chains of tyrants.

It was at the baths built by the Emperor Caracalla that he found hope for the future. The structure, erected by the cruelest of emperors, was crumbling; the bricks, mortared into place by slaves, pulled apart by the roots of fig trees and laurel. To Shelley, this exuberant and wild fecundity promised the inevitable victory over the tyranny of a nature that was fertile, democratic, and free, and he was inspired to write *Prometheus Unbound.*

In *American Ruins* we see how a dynamic, visible relationship with nature is critical to the potency of each ruin. Each has a unique, personal relationship to its environment—emphasized by an infrared technique that gives a greater luxuriance to nature and somehow shows the cracks and fissures in each stone. Looking back through these pages, we see Pueblo Bonito, the red rock of the Southwest, and the damp weeds and scrub on the balustrades of Bannerman Castle. At Windsor grasses sprout on the old walls, and the columns are said to create a music in the wind. But the most poetic example of how nature revives ruins is at Mission San Juan Capistrano in California, where the swallows return each March; for cliff-nesting birds, the walls of ruins are an ideal substitute. The church collapsed in an earthquake one Sunday morning in 1812, and forty-two worshipers were crushed and killed. Thousands of people come to watch the swallows return each year, and when the birds wheel, turn, and swoop, the ruin is a happy place. To Arthur Drooker, ruin is not the end of the story of a building but, rather, an episode in the cycle of the life, death, and reincarnation of great buildings. His photographs preserve the beauty, hope, and complexity of that phase.

Mission San Juan Capistrano, San Juan Capistrano, California

THE EAST

HARPERS FERRY *Harpers Ferry, West Virginia (1851–88)*

Located at the confluence of the Potomac and Shenandoah rivers, where the states of Maryland, Virginia, and West Virginia meet, Harpers Ferry was destined to become a bustling town, a strategic location during the Civil War, and a victim of nature's wrath. Though many structures in the historic district have been restored, a few ruins remain to remind one of Harpers Ferry's turbulent past.

St. John's Church was built in 1851–52. For part of the Civil War, it served as a Confederate barracks and hospital. The church sustained severe damage during the conflict and was rebuilt in 1882. Owing to declining attendance, St. John's was sold in 1895 and later abandoned.

The Shenandoah Pulp Factory, constructed in 1887–88, provided wood pulp for the paper industry. At its peak in the 1920s, the mill produced 15 tons of ground wood pulp daily. After several unprofitable years, it closed in 1935. A record flood in 1936 destroyed the mill.

The masonry piers in the Potomac River once supported the B&O Railroad Bridge. The radical abolitionist John Brown crossed an early version of this span when he led his raid on the arsenal here in October 1859. During the Civil War, the bridge was destroyed and replaced nine times. The last version, completed in 1870, was destroyed in the flood of 1936.

Masonry piers are also all that remain of the wagon bridge that spanned the Shenandoah River. Erected in 1882, it was swept away in a flood seven years later. After being rebuilt, it was taken down again in the flood of 1936.

The ruins stand within the Harpers Ferry National Historical Park.

▪ PAGES 20–21: *Bannerman Castle, Pollepel Island, New York*

■ *Wagon Bridge*

■ OPPOSITE AND ABOVE: *St. John's Church*

▮ ABOVE: *B&O Railroad Bridge pilings* ▮ OPPOSITE: *Sluiceways, Shenandoah Pulp Factory*

RENWICK *Roosevelt Island, New York City, New York (1856)*

Renwick has the distinction of being the only designated landmark ruin in New York City.

Initially completed in 1856, Smallpox Hospital, as it was then known, was the first institution in the country to treat victims of contagion and plague. Before this facility, the island treated smallpox patients in wooden shacks along the East River.

The hospital was made of stone quarried on the island. Construction workers were all inmates at a nearby penitentiary. The Gothic Revival structure cost $38,000 to build.

In 1886 Smallpox Hospital was converted into one of America's earliest schools of nursing. From 1902 to 1905 the school added the northern and southern wings. The building was abandoned in the early 1950s.

The ruin is named for its celebrated architect, James Renwick Jr., whose best-known work is St. Patrick's Cathedral on Manhattan's Fifth Avenue.

The Roosevelt Island Operating Corporation owns Renwick. A redevelopment plan proposes a garden and café in the stabilized ruins.

THE RUIN IS NAMED FOR ITS CELEBRATED ARCHITECT, JAMES RENWICK JR., WHOSE BEST-KNOWN WORK IS ST. PATRICK'S CATHEDRAL ON MANHATTAN'S FIFTH AVENUE.

BANNERMAN CASTLE *Pollepel Island, New York (1901)*

In 1900 Francis Bannerman VI, proprietor of the nation's largest military surplus store, purchased Pollepel Island, about 50 miles (80 km) north of New York City, to warehouse goods for his expanding inventory. The following year construction began on Bannerman's Island Arsenal, now the Hudson River Valley's premier ruin.

An untrained architect, Bannerman sketched his plans on scraps of paper and the backs of envelopes. He took as his inspiration European castles, especially those in his native Scotland. None of the island's buildings has right angles, possibly because Bannerman thought they would appear to be larger that way.

The complex included a lodge for workers and a family residence. Inside three arsenals, Bannerman stored his vast surplus from the Spanish–American War (1898), including saddles, rifles, uniforms, and other military goods. His loyal customers ranged from national armies to theatrical production companies.

The island's most distinctive structure was the tower, also known as "the Castle," a massive, five-story building perched high above the complex. At various times its bottom floors served as an arsenal and a chicken coop, while one of the upper floors was used to stretch sail material. Bannerman may have intended the tower to house a weapons museum.

Construction on the island ceased with Bannerman's death in 1918. Two years later, a major explosion of shells and powder destroyed some of the structures. By the 1960s rising maintenance and repair costs forced the Bannerman family to abandon the island and seek a buyer. The Smithsonian Institute acquired much of the surplus. In 1967 the State of New York bought the property. Left unattended, the complex fell victim to vandals and the elements. A fire of mysterious origin reduced the arsenal to ruin in 1969.

The Bannerman Castle Trust preserves the remaining structures and presents them collectively as a historical and cultural landmark.

■ *Arsenals 1 and 3 and Tower*

■ OPPOSITE: *Sally port* ■ ABOVE: *Terrace, family residence*

■ ABOVE: *Family residence* ■ OPPOSITE: *Arsenal 3*

BETHLEHEM STEEL MILL *Bethlehem, Pennsylvania (1904)*

The rusting blast furnaces that loom over this Lehigh Valley town once forged the steel that built a nation and made Bethlehem Steel a giant of American industry.

Founded in 1904, the Bethlehem Steel Corporation was the first company in the nation to produce the I-beam and wide-flange structural shapes, revolutionizing the construction industry. Bethlehem produced the steel used to build the Empire State Building, Rockefeller Center, Madison Square Garden, and the Golden Gate Bridge.

During both world wars, Bethlehem Steel was a major supplier of armor plate and ordnance to the U.S. armed forces. Many of the navy's fighting ships also used armor plate and large-caliber guns supplied by Bethlehem.

After more than a century of metal production at its Bethlehem plant, the company ceased operations in 1995. The demise of this industrial giant became a prominent example of the U.S. economy's transition away from industrial manufacturing and its inability to compete with cheap foreign labor.

Redevelopment plans call for the conversion of the vacant mill into a mixed-use site that will include shops, housing complexes, a casino, and space for the National Museum of Industrial History.

THE SOUTH

ROSEWELL *Gloucester, Virginia (1725)*

"I reflect often with pleasure on the philosophical evenings at Rosewell," recalled Thomas Jefferson.[1] John Page, grandson of the builder, attended the College of William & Mary with Jefferson. Later, the two patriots and lifelong friends often met here to discuss politics and indulge their mutual interest in astronomy by gazing at the heavens through a telescope in Rosewell's cupola.

John had been given Rosewell, its nearly 3,000 acres (1,200 ha), and numerous slaves, as a gift from his father, Mann Page II. Construction on the home began in about 1725 and was completed in the late 1730s. Rosewell was unlike any other house in the Tidewater region of Virginia. Shaped like a massive, three-story cube, with stone ornaments, rubbed brickwork, and recessed window frames, it was probably inspired by fashionable homes in London.

After a century of ownership by the Page family, Rosewell went through several hands before Josiah Deans bought it in 1853. During the Civil War, slaves continued to toil in Rosewell's fields and worked as house servants. The Deans family and their heirs owned Rosewell for more than 125 years.

An accidental fire destroyed the house on March 24, 1916. For descendants of Rosewell's slaves, the mansion had become a powerful symbol of a painful past. While neighbors attempted to extinguish the flames, one slave descendant reportedly paused in his nearby field, glared at the plume of smoke, and said, "Let it burn."[2]

The mansion's walls were left to decay under a growing tangle of vegetation. In 1979 descendants of the Deans family donated Rosewell to the Gloucester Historical Society and preservation work began in earnest. Since 1995 the Rosewell Foundation has taken on the mission of preserving and presenting this historic ruin.

■ PAGES 46–47: *Bulow Plantation, Bunnell, Florida*

BULOW PLANTATION *Bunnell, Florida (1821)*

The early nineteenth century marked a violent era in Florida history as settlers, including the Bulow family, established themselves on land that the Seminole Indians believed belonged to them.

In 1821 Major Charles Wilhelm Bulow acquired a large tract of wilderness in east Florida. Using slave labor, he cleared 2,200 acres (890 ha), planted sugar and other crops, and established a plantation bearing his name. When Major Bulow died at age forty-four, he left all his holdings to his only son, John.

Under John's skilled management, the Bulow Plantation prospered until the outbreak of the Second Seminole War in 1835. John, like other settlers in the area, opposed the U.S. government's intention to remove the Seminoles to reservations west of the Mississippi River.

He demonstrated his disapproval by ordering a cannon to be fired on state militiamen entering his property. Troops took Bulow prisoner, but after an unsuccessful campaign, they relocated to St. Augustine. When the Indians became more hostile, Bulow abandoned his plantation and followed the troops northward.

In January 1836 the Seminoles burned Bulow and other plantations in the area. Discouraged by the destruction, John Bulow went to Paris, where he died three months later, at the age of twenty-six.

A sugar mill, the only remaining structure, stands in the Bulow Plantation Ruins Historic State Park, operated by the Florida Department of Environmental Protection, Division of Recreation and Parks.

IN JANUARY 1836 THE SEMINOLES BURNED BULOW PLANTATION. DISCOURAGED BY ITS DESTRUCTION, JOHN BULOW WENT TO PARIS, WHERE HE DIED THREE MONTHS LATER, AT THE AGE OF TWENTY-SIX.

OLD GOVERNOR'S MANSION *Barboursville, Virginia (1822)*

In 1814 Virginia governor James Barbour asked his friend Thomas Jefferson to design a home in the same style as Monticello. Jefferson was not only the author of the Declaration of Independence and the nation's third president but also an amateur architect. Monticello, Jefferson's Neoclassical residence near Charlottesville, was his "essay on architecture."

Jefferson's inspiration was Andrea Palladio, the sixteenth-century Italian architect whose system of proportion was based on Classical models. Jefferson described Palladio's *I quattro libri dell'architettura* as his "bible." He had based his other noteworthy design, the Rotunda at the University of Virginia, on the Pantheon in Rome, which had also influenced Palladio.

In his plan for Barbour's residence, Jefferson again followed Palladian principles of order and harmony. His design included five bedrooms, a library, a dining room, and his signature feature, an octagon-shaped drawing room.

The Barbour family moved into the brick manor in 1822. By then, James represented Virginia in the U.S. Senate. Later, he became secretary of war and ambassador to the court of St. James under President John Quincy Adams.

At his death in 1842, Barbour bequeathed the mansion to his heirs, who occupied it until an accidental fire destroyed the house on Christmas Day 1884.

The stabilized ruins are on land owned by Barboursville Vineyards, a Virginia winery.

THE COTTAGE   *East Baton Rouge Parish, Louisiana (1824)*

Colonel Abner Duncan built the Cottage in 1824 as a wedding gift for his daughter and her husband, Frederick Daniel Conrad. As an early example of Greek Revival architecture, the twenty-two-room mansion was considered one of the finest homes in the Baton Rouge area. Visitors included Jefferson Davis, Henry Clay, Zachary Taylor, and the Marquis de Lafayette.

Prior to the Civil War, the plantation flourished. The Conrads amassed great wealth from sugar and cotton. The conflict would change their fortunes. Union troops occupied the Cottage and used it as a hospital to treat soldiers with yellow fever. Those who died from the disease were buried in the grounds. The family abandoned the property after the war.

A few years later, Frederick Conrad died in New Orleans. A tutor who had taught the Conrad children returned to the vacant mansion and lived there as a recluse until his death. As years passed, the Cottage again stood empty.

In the 1920s Conrad's descendants began a restoration of the house, which had remained fairly intact. It was opened to the public in the 1950s as a museum. The mansion burned to the ground in February 1960.

The ruins sit on private property along the River Road near Plaquemine.

AS AN EARLY EXAMPLE OF GREEK REVIVAL

ARCHITECTURE, THE COTTAGE WAS CONSIDERED

ONE OF THE FINEST HOMES IN THE BATON

ROUGE AREA.

SHELDON CHURCH *Gardens Corner, South Carolina (1826)*

The Church of Prince William's Parish, better known as Sheldon, was once considered one of the finest houses of worship in the colony of South Carolina. It followed the Neoclassical style, with Doric columns, massive walls, and arches. It was named for the ancestral home of William Bull and his family in Warwickshire, England.

Construction began in 1745 on land donated by Bull. The church was finished in 1755 and featured an equestrian statue of Prince William and a fountain in which Bull had his slaves baptized. When Bull died later that year, after having served as the colony's lieutenant governor, he was buried in the church grounds.

According to local lore, the Prince William statue was melted and made into bullets during the War of Independence, and one of the church's vaults was used to store weapons. In retribution for the rebellion, British troops marching on Charleston burned the church in 1779.

Sheldon was rebuilt in 1826. Though not restored to its original glory, it remained home to hundreds of congregants until the Civil War. In 1865 General William Tecumseh Sherman's troops torched Sheldon as they stormed through the Carolinas after their historic March to the Sea.

St. Helena's Episcopal Church eventually bought the land on which the ruins are located. It holds annual services there on the second Sunday after Easter.

WINDSOR *Alcorn, Mississippi (1859)*

Windsor was the largest antebellum Greek Revival home in Mississippi. It served as the residence of Smith Coffee Daniell II, a wealthy cotton planter, and his family.

Building began in 1859, with slave labor undertaking basic construction. Skilled carpenters from New England finished the interior woodwork. Ironworks in St. Louis manufactured the stairs, column capitals, and balustrades and shipped them down the Mississippi River to the site. The total cost of construction was about $175,000, more than $3 million today.

When completed in 1861, Windsor featured twenty-nine Corinthian columns, each 45 feet (14 m) tall, and twenty-three rooms, including two residential floors. Innovations included a dumbwaiter connecting the dining room with the kitchen, located in the basement. Tanks in the attic provided water for two bathrooms, a rarity at the time.

Smith Daniell lived in his grand home only a few weeks before he died at age thirty-four. His wife and three children stayed on despite the loss of many of the family's holdings during the Civil War. In the conflict, both sides used Windsor's cupola as an observation post. Union forces turned the mansion into a hospital during the Battle of Port Gibson in May 1863.

Windsor survived the war only to be destroyed by a fire on February 17, 1890, after a guest left a lighted cigar on the upper balcony. All was lost except the columns and ironwork.

Descendants of the Daniell family donated Windsor to the State of Mississippi in 1974. The Mississippi Department of Archives and History maintains this classic southern ruin.

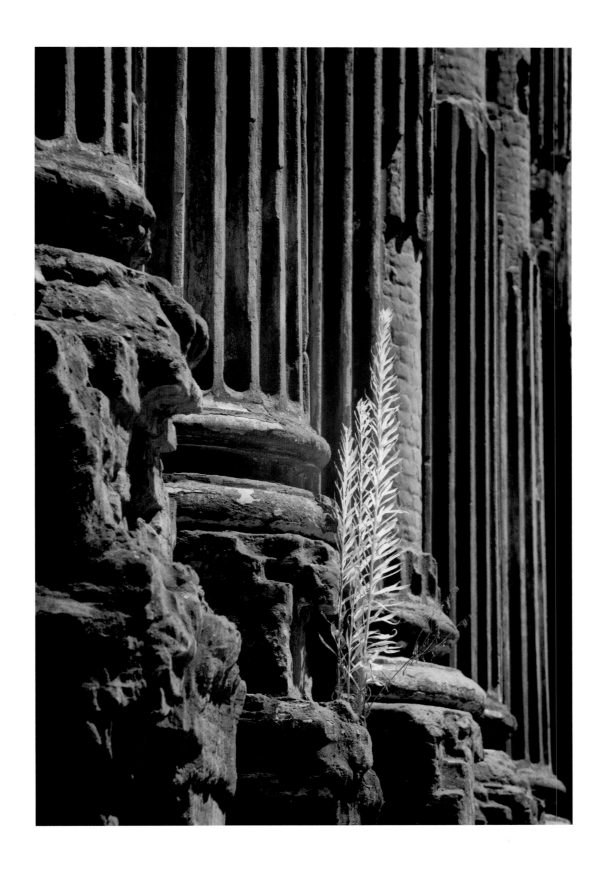

DUNGENESS *Cumberland Island, Georgia (late 1880s)*

In 1881 Thomas Carnegie, the younger brother of industrialist Andrew Carnegie, and his wife, Lucy, visited Cumberland Island off the coast of Georgia. Enchanted with its natural beauty, the couple purchased land to build a winter home.

The Carnegies began construction of their estate on the ruins of the former home of Nathaniel Greene, a Revolutionary War general, and retained the property's name, Dungeness. Thomas died suddenly in 1886, leaving his wife to complete the mansion.

The new Dungeness was the epitome of Gilded Age opulence. It was so big that ships' captains used it as a navigation point. The fifty-nine-room turreted castle boasted an indoor pool, a billiard parlor, a squash court, and a golf course. Fruit orchards flourished. Wild game, brought from the mainland, roamed the property. In such splendor, Lucy Carnegie entertained family and friends from Pittsburgh.

Lucy continued to develop Cumberland, eventually purchasing 90 percent of the island and building homes for family members. When she died in 1916, she stipulated that no lands were to be sold while her nine children were still alive.

By 1925 Dungeness proved too costly to maintain, and the family left the property in the care of an overseer. Disputes over the estate's game led to its demise. In 1959 an overseer shot and injured a poacher. Soon after, Dungeness burned in a fire of mysterious origin. No evidence directly linking anyone to the crime was ever found, and no one was charged.

In 1972 the property became part of the Cumberland Island National Seashore.

THE SOUTHWEST

ANASAZI RUINS

Canyon de Chelly, Arizona (AD 300–1200)

This stunning red-rock canyon got its name from the Spanish/English corruption of *tseyi*, a Navajo word for "into the rock" or "rock wall." More than a thousand years ago, the Anasazi (Ancient Ones) built multistory villages and compounds in alcoves beneath walls that rise more than 1,000 feet (300 m) above the canyon floor. These ruins attest to the architectural ingenuity of the earliest Native Americans.

The White House Ruin, named for the whitewashed walls of the central room in the upper level of this village, dates from about 1200. The Navajo mention this ruin in their Night Chant, calling it *Kinii Na'igai* (White House In Between) because of this unique coloring. At its peak, White House was home to about one hundred people in some sixty rooms constructed of stone blocks and mud mortar.

Antelope House Ruin is named for nineteenth-century Navajo paintings on a nearby cliff wall. Building commenced around 700 and continued intermittently for nearly six hundred years. Most of the remaining structures were constructed after 1050, some as late as 1250.

Mummy Cave Ruin is one of the largest ancient dwellings in Canyon de Chelly. Its tower rises three stories. The ruin takes its name from two well-preserved mummies archaeologists discovered there. Its traditional Navajo name is *Tseyaa Kini* (House Under Rock). Construction began around 300, making Mummy Cave one of the earliest sites in the canyon.

The Anasazi ruins are located in Canyon de Chelly National Monument.

■ PAGES 84–85: *Pueblo Bonito, Chaco Canyon, New Mexico* ■ OPPOSITE: *White House Ruin*

■ ABOVE AND OPPOSITE: *Antelope House Ruin*

■ OPPOSITE AND ABOVE: *Mummy Cave Ruin*

THE GREAT HOUSES *Chaco Canyon, New Mexico (AD 850–1150)*

More than a thousand years ago, Chaco Canyon was the center of a flourishing society of native peoples. Its large-scale architecture, complex social organization, and extensive trade network created a distinctive cultural vision.

The rise of the Chacoan people began in the mid-800s and lasted more than three hundred years. The Chacoans built Great Houses, massive stone buildings, using masonry techniques unique to the period. These dwellings rose several stories and contained hundreds of rooms. It took decades, even centuries, to construct some of these buildings.

During the middle to late 800s, these enterprising people began erecting the Great Houses of Pueblo Bonito, Chetro Ketl, Pueblo del Arroyo, and others. These structures were often oriented to celestial points and cardinal directions, suggesting that the Chacoans possessed a deep understanding of the cosmos.

By 1050 Chaco had become the commercial and cultural hub of the San Juan Basin. Roads connecting to other Great Houses in the region extended Chaco's influence far beyond the local community.

Beginning in the 1100s, Chaco's role as a regional center declined. The people migrated to new areas and interacted with other cultures. Their descendants are today's southwestern Native Americans. Many of them still consider Chaco a sacred and spiritual place.

The ruins are located in Chaco Culture National Historical Park.

■ *Kin Kletso*

■ OPPOSITE: *Pueblo del Arroyo* ■ ABOVE: *Pueblo Bonito*

■ OPPOSITE: *Chetro Ketl* ■ ABOVE: *Pueblo Bonito*

HOVENWEEP *Colorado–Utah border (MID-1100S–1300)*

The square, circular, and D-shaped towers that form the skyline of Hovenweep remain some of the most unusual examples of ancestral Puebloan architecture.

Some towers were built as early as the mid-1100s, but most were erected after 1230 and were inhabited for about a generation. Many of them are situated directly on the edge of a canyon or atop isolated boulders. It took skillful masonry to construct lasting structures in such precarious locations.

Archaeologists have advanced several theories to explain the use of the buildings at Hovenweep. The distinctive towers might have been celestial observatories, defensive positions, storage facilities, ceremonial gathering places, or private dwellings. Their exact purpose remains unknown.

By 1300 the inhabitants had departed for what are now Arizona and New Mexico. Why they left also lacks a definitive explanation. Some suggest that drought or depletion of natural resources may have caused their disappearance. Others speculate that conflict could have prompted the evacuation.

In 1854 W. D. Huntington, the leader of a Mormon expedition in southeastern Utah, made the first report of these remarkable structures. Pioneer photographer William H. Jackson first used the name *Hovenweep*, a Paiute/Ute word meaning "deserted valley," to describe the area.

These mystifying ruins are located in Hovenweep National Monument.

■ *Hovenweep Castle*

■ OPPOSITE: *Eroded Boulder House* ■ ABOVE: *Stronghold House*

▪ ABOVE: *Cajon* ▪ OPPOSITE: *Twin Towers*

FORT UNION *Watrous, New Mexico (1863)*

This frontier outpost was established in 1851 to guard the Santa Fe Trail. It protected American traders and travelers from Indian attacks and other threats. During its forty-year history, three different forts were constructed close together. The third Fort Union, erected between 1863 and 1869, was the largest in the American Southwest and functioned as a military garrison, a territorial arsenal, and a supply depot. More than an army post, Fort Union was a bustling symbol of westward expansion.

The chimneys mark the site of the nine homes on Officers' Row. The post commander lived in the center house, which was also the most spacious. Construction began in 1864 and was completed three years later. Designed in the Territorial Style, with adobe walls and a stone foundation, each residence had a front porch and a backyard. The row served as the fort's social center, playing host to teas, dances, and weddings.

At the Mechanics Corral, civilian workers repaired mostly military wagons. The corral housed shops for blacksmiths, wheelwrights, and carpenters. It was the scene of intense labor as freight wagons, trader caravans, and stagecoaches traveling the trail's two main thoroughfares, the Mountain Branch and the Cimarron Cutoff, converged on Fort Union.

When the Santa Fe Trail gave way to the Santa Fe Railroad, Fort Union's importance declined. The army gradually phased out the fort's supply operations and closed the depot in 1883. By 1891 the fort was abandoned.

The ruins stand in Fort Union National Monument.

Officers' Row

■ OPPOSITE: *Officers' Row*   ■ ABOVE: *Mechanics Corral*

RHYOLITE *Rhyolite, Nevada (1904)*

When two prospectors, Shorty Harris and Ed Cross, struck gold in the Nevada desert in August 1904, the rush to Rhyolite was on. Named for the deposits of the mineral that contained much of the gold, the town supported a population of more than ten thousand at its peak in 1907.

The *Rhyolite Herald,* one of three local newspapers, proclaimed, "Rhyolite is awakening! Are you a live one or a dead one? We have no room here for the man who won't make a hustle for the good of his own town."[1] This was no idle boast. In its heyday, Rhyolite had electricity, plumbing, a telephone service, an opera house, a stock exchange, a train station, and two hospitals. It also had an extensive red-light district that drew women from as far away as San Francisco.

The financial panic of 1907 initiated Rhyolite's decline. In the following years, the mines shut down and banks and businesses failed. By 1919 everyone had moved on, and the boomtown became a ghost town.

Many of Rhyolite's buildings were constructed of permanent materials such as concrete and brick, not just the canvas and wood that typified most mining-town structures.

Rhyolite's ruins include the concrete remnants of its tallest building, the John S. Cook Bank, built for $90,000; the Overbury Building, which housed the Rhyolite National Bank; the Porter Brothers' Store, which had the slogan "We handle all things but whiskey"; and a school, the last major structure built in the town.

Rhyolite is located 2½ miles (4 km) west of Beatty, Nevada.

■ *John S. Cook Bank*

■ OPPOSITE AND ABOVE: *Overbury Building*

■ *Porter Brothers' Store*

THE FINANCIAL PANIC OF 1907 INITIATED

RHYOLITE'S DECLINE. BY 1919 EVERYONE HAD

MOVED ON, AND THE BOOMTOWN BECAME A

GHOST TOWN.

THE MISSIONS *(1622–1720)*

Catholic orders established missions across the Southwest to spread their faith among native peoples and acculturate them to Spanish ways. The missions served not only the cross but also the crown, aiding the expansion of the Spanish empire.

Native Americans built the missions under the guidance of skilled craftsmen. Within their protective walls stood a church, a *convento* (priests' quarters), a plaza, and workshops. Life resembled that of Spanish villages. When not praying to their new god, the neophytes learned vocational skills to sustain the missions' economies.

The need for missions diminished on account of the effects of European diseases, assimilation, intermarriage, and environmental pressures. Eventually, they were abandoned.

The chain of missions established along the San Antonio River in the eighteenth century formed the largest concentration of Catholic missions in North America. The first of these, Mission San Antonio de Valero, founded in 1718, later became known as "the Alamo," the site of the most famous battle of the Texas Revolution (1835–36). It's now under the care of the Daughters of the Republic of Texas. Mission San Jose, the largest in the chain, was a major social center and enjoyed its reputation as "Queen of the Missions." San Jose and three other missions are located within the San Antonio Missions National Historical Park.

Abo and Quarai are two architecturally distinctive missions in New Mexico. Abo, established in 1622, features a sophisticated buttressing technique, rare for seventeenth-century North American structures. While Abo and Quarai have similar elements, they are quite unlike any other mission ruins found in the Southwest. They're located in the Salinas Pueblo Missions National Monument.

The mission at Pecos, New Mexico, was the scene of violence during the Pueblo Revolt of 1680, perhaps the largest rebellion of its kind. Pueblo Indians, resistant to Spanish rule, killed a priest and destroyed the church. A replacement church was built in 1717. Its ruin is part of the Pecos National Historical Park.

Abo Mission, Mountainair, New Mexico

■ ABOVE: *Pecos Mission, Pecos, New Mexico*   ■ OPPOSITE: *Quarai Mission, Mountainair, New Mexico*

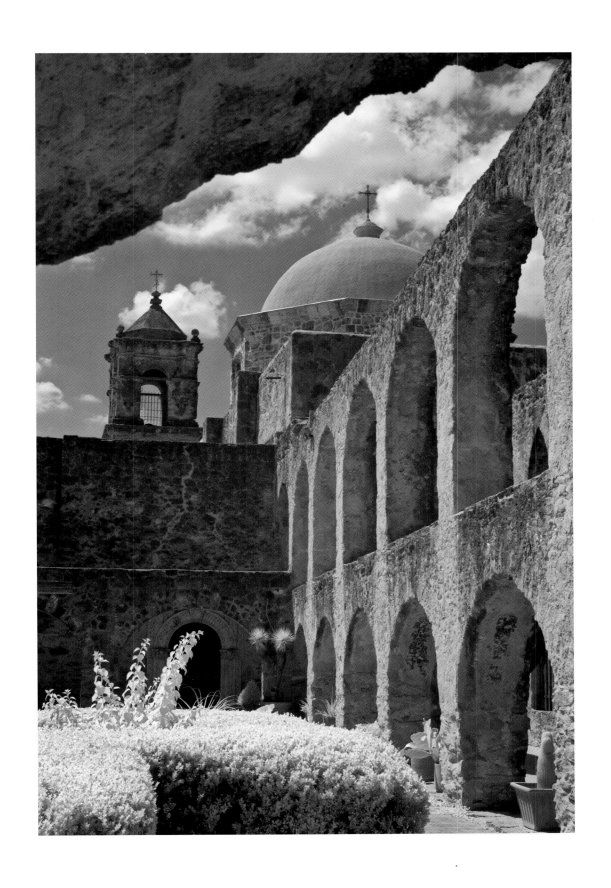

■ OPPOSITE: *Mission San Antonio de Valero ("the Alamo"), San Antonio, Texas* ■ ABOVE: *Mission San Jose, San Antonio, Texas*

CALIFORNIA AND HAWAII

KANIAKAPUPU *Nuuanu Valley, Oahu, Hawaii (1845)*

North of downtown Honolulu, hidden in the lush vegetation of the Nuuanu Valley, stand the remains of Kaniakapupu, the summer estate of King Kamehameha III and his queen, Kalama.

Kaniakapupu (Sound of the Land Snails) was completed by 1845. Its design represented a transition between Hawaiian and nineteenth-century Western architecture. It measured 40 by 45 feet (13 × 14 m), had a thatched roof, a raised wooden floor, framed glazed windows, and walls made of coral and stone.

Here the king hosted grand entertainments. The largest of these was a luau attended by an estimated ten thousand people on July 31, 1847, to celebrate Sovereignty Restoration Day, an event marking the restoration of the Hawaiian Kingdom after it was forced under British rule for five months in 1843. Foreign guests, unaccustomed to sitting on mats with the natives, sat at tables in the main house. Outside, the royal party

and the multitudes feasted at a long lanai, or porch. They dined on pork, salt fish, coconuts, and other island delicacies.

It is believed that the site was in ruins by 1873, having suffered from years of exposure to the elements. The crumbling walls of the main house are all that remain.

Preservation efforts began in the 1950s, when the Territorial Commission on Historic Sites cleared and stabilized the ruins. Lack of maintenance caused further deterioration for the next thirty years. In 1998 the Historic Hawaii Foundation established a fund to restabilize the ruins, a task completed two years later. An archaeological survey continues.

The State Historic Preservation Division of Hawaii's Department of Land and Natural Resources oversees Kaniakapupu with the involvement of the Historic Hawaii Foundation and other local preservation organizations.

Kaniakapupu is located at the end of an unmarked trail off the Pali Highway.

■ PAGES 120–121: *Kaniakapupu, Nuuanu Valley, Oahu, Hawaii*

WOLF HOUSE *Glen Ellen, California (1911)*

"My house will be standing, act of God permitting, for a thousand years," declared Jack London. Sadly for the world-famous author of *The Call of the Wild* and numerous other books and short stories, it was not to be.

London lived a life as colorful as the ones he wrote about. At various times he was a hobo, a gold prospector, a war correspondent, and a sailor. It would take a special place to entice the wandering writer to settle down. He found it in the Sonoma Valley. In 1905 he purchased more than 100 acres (40 ha) there and established the Beauty Ranch. Its centerpiece would be, in London's words, a "lofty lodge."

Construction began in 1911. The lodge was built to last and to blend in with its environment. Building materials included unpeeled redwood logs, lava rocks, and Spanish tile. The floors were made of thick concrete slabs to withstand fire, floods, and earthquakes. The home, dubbed Wolf House by London's friends, covered 15,000 square feet (1,400 sq. m), rose four stories, had twenty-six rooms, nine fireplaces, and a reflecting pool in the courtyard.

On August 22, 1913, a month before London and his wife, Charmian, were to move in, a fire destroyed the home. "It was a quick fire," London recalled. "We can't tell if it was incendiary or not. The walls are standing and I shall rebuild."[1] Lacking funds, London never rebuilt his dream house.

In 1995 forensic experts concluded that the fire was caused by the spontaneous combustion of linseed oil–soaked rags left by construction workers.

The Wolf House ruins stand within the Jack London State Historic Park, operated by the California Department of Parks and Recreation.

KNAPP'S CASTLE *Santa Barbara, California (1916)*

In 1912 George Owen Knapp, a retired, but hardly retiring, Union Carbide executive, moved to Santa Barbara, California. The coastal community was then just a small town hemmed in by the Santa Ynez Mountains. Undeterred by this imposing geological obstacle, Knapp spent millions from his personal fortune to help build a road along the ridgeline, paving the way for cars and further development.

During construction, Knapp fell in love with the spectacular views of the Santa Ynez Valley. In 1916 he purchased 160 acres (65 ha) and vowed "to make the tract a private mountain lodge that in natural beauty and grandeur will have few to equal it on the American continent."[1]

Knapp employed more than twenty men to build his lodge, including Italian stonemasons, who laid down native sandstone to form foundations, walls, and fireplaces. When completed in 1920, Knapp's castle had seven buildings in all. The main house had five bedrooms, a dining room, an observatory, and a room for Knapp's other passion, his pipe organ. In addition to the main house, he built a studio, a workman's cottage, a staff dormitory, and a superintendent's house. Water was pumped from waterfalls near the property to a reservoir above the lodge.

In 1940 Ms. Francis Holden purchased the castle. Just five weeks after she moved in, a forest fire cut through the property and destroyed most of the buildings. Only the observatory remained. The castle was never rebuilt because of the exorbitant cost. Another forest fire claimed the observatory in 1964, and with that, the last of Knapp's Castle succumbed to the elements.

The ruins sit on private property off Highway 154, near Santa Barbara, California.

KNAPP VOWED "TO MAKE THE TRACT A PRIVATE MOUNTAIN LODGE THAT IN NATURAL BEAUTY AND GRANDEUR WILL HAVE FEW TO EQUAL IT ON THE AMERICAN CONTINENT."

U.S. PENITENTIARY AT ALCATRAZ *Alcatraz Island, California (1934)*

An eighteenth-century Spanish explorer named it *Isla de los Alcatraces* (Island of the Pelicans), but most people know Alcatraz simply as "the Rock." It has served as a fort, a military prison, and a federal penitentiary that housed infamous criminals such as Al "Scarface" Capone, Machine Gun Kelly, and Doc Barker. Increasing maintenance and operating costs forced the closure of the prison in 1963. The ruins resonate with Alcatraz's legacy of hard time.

The Warden's House, a Mission Revival–style home, had seventeen rooms with sweeping views of the bay. Built in the 1920s, it was originally the home of the military prison commandant. When Alcatraz became a federal penitentiary in 1934, the first of four wardens and their families occupied it. A trusted inmate served as both gardener and houseboy. In June 1970 a fire swept through the abandoned building, leaving only the shell.

The Alcatraz Post Exchange (PX), or "Soldiers' Clubhouse," built in 1910, was the local general store for soldiers and their families. When Alcatraz became a federal penitentiary, the PX was converted into a recreation hall and officers' club, with a dance floor, a gym, a bowling alley, and a soda fountain. It was one of several buildings, including the Warden's House, that was destroyed by fire in 1970.

The piles of rubble in the Parade Ground are the remains of the correctional officers' apartments. Crews from the General Services Administration bulldozed these structures in the wake of a nineteen-month occupation by Indians of All Tribes, a political organization seeking restoration of native lands, that began in 1969.

In 1972 Alcatraz was designated part of the Golden Gate National Recreation Area.

■ *Warden's House*

■ OPPOSITE AND ABOVE: *Post Exchange*

■ OPPOSITE AND ABOVE: *Parade Ground*

ACKNOWLEDGMENTS ARTHUR DROOKER

THIS BOOK WOULD NOT HAVE BEEN POSSIBLE without the support and involvement of many people. To them, I owe a deep debt of gratitude, and I proudly acknowledge their contributions.

Michelle Dunn Marsh, director of Aperture West, was the first photography professional to express enthusiasm for this series. Her early endorsement gave me the motivation to pursue *American Ruins* as a project with serious potential.

Mary Virginia Swanson, legendary consultant to photographers, gave me invaluable guidance. She played a vital role in helping me transform the idea of *American Ruins* into a successful proposal for publication and exhibition.

Gary Chassman, president of Verve Editions, produced this book with the sensitivity of an artist and the precision of a diamond cutter. No detail escapes his attention, and every detail goes into making not just a book but also a journey that engages the reader's imagination. I look forward to working with him again. I'm also thankful to Gary's able project manager, Eliza Shanley.

R. Mac Holbert, cofounder of Nash Editions in Manhattan Beach, California, performed the imaging of the pictures that appear in *American Ruins*. Perhaps no one has done more to advance the cause of digital imaging and printmaking than Mac. Valued friend, consultant, and collaborator, he has made me a better photographer.

Kari Finkler, designer, put this book together with consummate skill and visionary talent. In preparing for publication, I always looked forward to seeing her layouts, knowing they would go far beyond anything I could imagine and would inspire me to do my best in return.

The unsung heroes of this book are those vigilant few who preserve the ruins featured in these pages. I sing the praises of those who were especially helpful to me: Neil Caplan, president of the Bannerman Castle Trust; Mike Bowman and Dan Doyal of the New York State Office of Parks, Recreation and Historic Preservation; Hilarie M. Hicks, executive director of the Rosewell Foundation, and her associate Mary Warren; Judith Berdy, president of the Roosevelt Island Historical Society; Vince Taylor, park superintendent of the Sweetwater Creek State Park, Georgia; and all the National Park Service rangers who work at the federally preserved historical parks and monuments featured in *American Ruins*. Their dedication ensures that these fragile national treasures will be there for generations to come.

I would also like to thank John Bilotta, Web-site designer extraordinaire, for all his help behind the scenes; Deborah Boyd, executive director of the New Smyrna Beach Visitors Bureau, for her assistance and hospitality; Theo Anderson, a gifted photographer, and the good folks at the Banana Factory in Bethlehem, Pennsylvania, for letting me tag along on their shoot at the steel mill; Doug Durand Jr. and Kevin McQuade for their site suggestions; and Lis Rawlins for being a good neighbor.

Perhaps most difficult to thank adequately are those friends and family who actively demonstrated their support for this project. Special mention goes to my sister, Sandy Drooker, and to dear friends Diane Arkenstone, Blair Bess, Jeff Fishman, Gary Foreman, Julie Harman, Paul Hutton, and Gary Ross.